This

Book

Belongs

To

_____

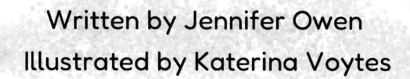

Written by Jennifer Owen

Illustrated by Katerina Voytes

Prince ~~Charming~~ KINDNESS

REDHAWK
PUBLICATIONS

In a small kingdom, there lives a boy who is known as **Prince Charming**... begins the Narrator.

"Excuse me, Narrator?" the Prince says.

Yes Prince?

"I don't want to be known as **Prince Charming**."

What shall you be known as then?

This is **your** story.

You must have a name.

"I don't know…" The Prince starts to wonder what he will be known as.

"Maybe we can continue the story and find the answer?" the Prince asks shyly.

The Narrator continues...

The young Prince decides to walk as he searches for an answer. As the Prince continues to wonder about his name, he notices someone...an elderly lady struggling to cross the street. The Prince rushes over to help.

The Prince helps the elderly lady make it safely to the sidewalk.

"That was kind. Thank you."

The lady pats the Prince on the head.

"You're welcome," replies the Prince.

They each continue on their way.

The Prince strolls through the park and sees kids playing together.

Then the Prince notices a girl playing hopscotch by herself.

He decides to ask if he can play, too.

"Can I play with you?" asks the Prince.

The girl brightens with a huge smile.
She begins to move her hands rapidly.

The Prince feels uncomfortable and wants to walk away.

Was this sign language?

He decides to try to understand.

She just wants to play, and so does he.

The Prince and the girl
are having fun playing
hopscotch together when
the girl's mother comes
over to take her home.

"Can you teach me some sign language?" he asks.

The mother shows the Prince how to sign "*thank you*" and "*friend*." As they walk away, the mother turns to the Prince,

"That was truly kind. Thank you."

"What do you mean?" asks the Prince.

"You wanted to learn her language," replies the mother.

"You're welcome," replies the Prince.

"Can we play again sometime?" asks the Prince.

The mother smiles and nods to the Prince.

"What's her name?" the Prince asks the mother.

"Abigail."

The Prince signs "*thank you*" and waves goodbye.

The Prince is happy he made a new friend, but he still wonders about his name.

"Narrator?" the Prince asks.

Yes, Prince?

The Prince begins to worry, "What if I can't find my name?"

Do not worry, Prince. You are closer to the answer than you think.

Keep looking.

"Ugh. What does that mean?" the Prince moans.

You will soon find the answer, replies the Narrator.

Now, shall we continue on the journey?

The Prince kicks at the gravel with frustration.

The Prince then notices a line waiting at an ice cream truck.

He loves ice cream, too!

The Prince decides to buy his own ice cream cone – a mint chocolate chip.

He is excited.

The father and son in front of him leave the truck with their strawberry ice cream.

The little boy accidentally drops his scoop and starts crying.

"I'm sorry, kiddo. That's all the cash I had."

The father comforts his son with a hug.

"I would like a strawberry ice cream cone, please" the Prince says to the ice cream man.

The Prince walks over carefully to the crying boy.

"I got you another ice cream cone," the Prince says.

The boy smiles happily at the Prince.

"That was kind. Thank you!" says the father.

"You're welcome," the Prince replies.

The Prince starts back home when he notices a book on the sidewalk.

He looks around and sees a teacher carrying a lot of items into the school.

"Excuse me!" shouts the Prince.

"I believe you dropped a book."

"Oh my! Thank you. That is truly kind," says the teacher.

"Can I help you?" asks the Prince.

The teacher responds, "I appreciate the offer, but I am okay now."

The Prince is confused that someone said no to help.

"Helping others is important," the Prince says in a soft voice.

"Yes indeed," the teacher responds. She then adds, "You must respect when someone says no. It's okay to not want help. However, don't let that discourage you from continuing to offer help to others."

The Prince smiles at the teacher and continues home.

The Prince arrives home to find his mother, the Queen, decorating a cake in the kitchen.

"Can I help, Mother?" asks the Prince.

"That is kind. Thank you." The mother kisses him on the cheek.

"Mom," the Prince groans.

They both start laughing.

"What did you do today?" his mother asks.

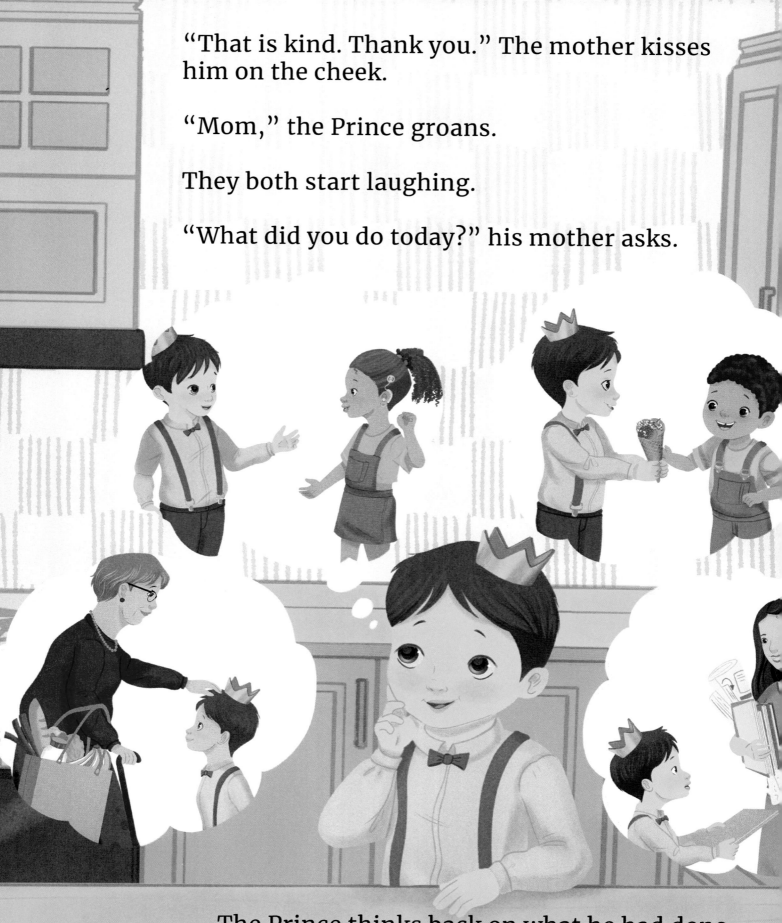

The Prince thinks back on what he had done.

"I was kind," states the Prince.

"That's my little man!" says his mother as they finish icing the cake.

The Prince's mother is enormously proud of him.

"You will make a fine King."

The Queen kisses her son on the cheek once more.

"Now, no eating the cake before tomorrow. It's for the special event."

"Can I invite a friend?" asks the Prince.

In a small kingdom, there lives a boy who is known as *Prince Kindness* ... begins the Narrator.

"I like the sound of that!" says Prince Kindness. He continues to dance with his new friend, Abigail.

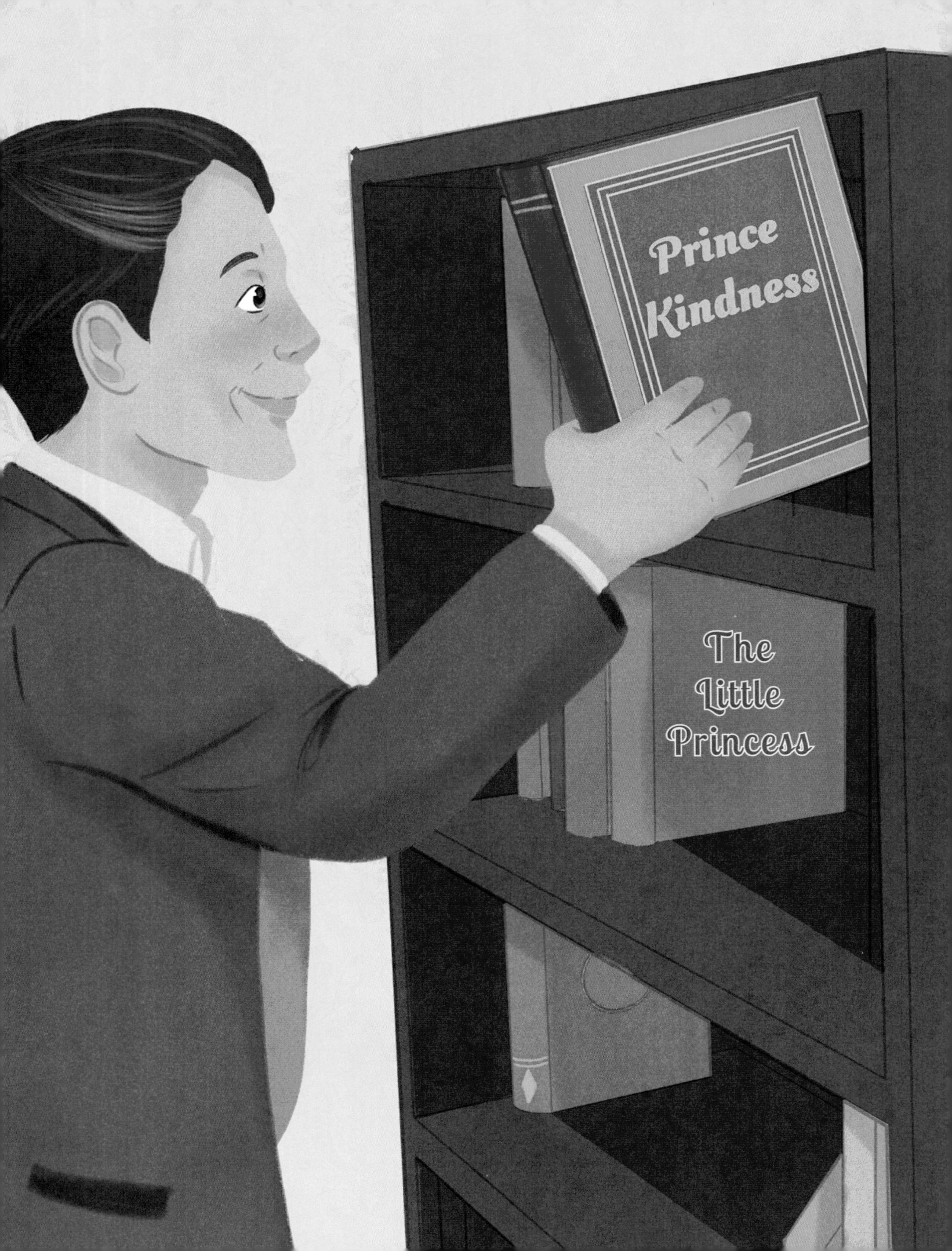
Prince Kindness
The Little Princess

"Narrator," comes a voice from down the hall.

Yes, Little Princess?

"My turn! My name," she says in distress.

She begins to wonder about **her** story.

To be continued...

Thank you to everyone who has supported me in this journey of becoming an author. I'd like to give a special shoutout to Tammie Canerday, Heather Hall, my brother, and most importantly, the little Prince himself, Bennett Miller, for inspiring the characters in this book. I would like to give gratitude to my mother and father for always inspiring me – I would not be where I am today without the support of my parents.

Thank you!

About the Author and Illustrator

Jennifer Owen

I grew up in the mountains of North Carolina and graduated from Lees–McRae College with a BA in Psychology and an MA in Child Development with a concentration in Administration and Special Needs from Erikson Institute.

I love being the creative, imaginative, and energetic person that I am! I write books with subtle messages about how we should treat one another with kindness and respect, honoring everyone's abilities and differences.

Katerina Voytes

More than anything, I love to draw children and their emotions. For over seven years, I have worked with authors all over the world, creating bright and positive books.

I like everything cute: Cats, dogs, and indeed, all animals.

I sincerely hope that children will enjoy my illustrations and that they will help make our world a little better.

Made in the USA
Middletown, DE
27 September 2023

39404319R00020